BACKYARD
CRITTERS & CREATURES

DISCOVER AN AMAZING KINGDOM OF CREATURES RIGHT OUTSIDE YOUR DOOR!

Words & Photography
by Cheryl Johnson

BACKYARD CRITTERS AND CREATURES

Written by Cheryl Johnson
Photography by Cheryl Johnson

Graphics by Cheryl Johnson

For rights and permissions, please contact:

Bird Nerd Publishing
www.BirdNerdPublishing.com

Are You Ready For An Amazing Adventure?

Look Up...

Look Down...

Look All Around...

And you'll be amazed at what you'll discover!

Did you know that there's a unique and exciting kingdom of critters and creatures just waiting to be discovered in your own backyard or park? Right outside your door is an entire ecosystem, where every living organism works together to create a healthy environment where all the creatures grow and prosper. These creatures come in every color of the rainbow and can be as small as your finger to as large as a dog. Many are hiding in plain sight, but with the right tools and skills, you can discover this amazing kingdom for yourself.

TOOLS
You're going to need some tools to make your adventure more fun:
- *Your eyes and your ears*
- *A notebook or paper to document your discoveries (see the back of this book for information about "My Nature Journal" - the perfect journal for kids to document their nature discoveries)*
- *Colored pencils or crayons*
- *A magnifying glass or binoculars*
- *Your sense of adventure*

REMEMBER - To all of the critters and creatures in your backyard or park, you look like a big, scary giant, and even though you might want to be friends, they might think you want to hurt them. If a creature feels scared they will try to protect themselves by hiding, and if that doesn't work, they might try to bite or sting you. That's why it's always a good idea to move slowly and don't try to touch or pick up any of your new backyard friends.

So come on, let's go see what we can discover!

DISCOVERY KEY

As you turn the pages of this book and discover some of the different creatures you might find in your backyard or park, use the Discover Key below to learn more about where the creature lives, when it's active, and when you might see it in your yard or park.

What part of the country it lives in

What time of year you can see it or when it's most active

Winter **Spring** **Summer** **Fall**

Is it more active during the day or at night

Diurnal **Nocturnal**

Where in your yard or park you're most likely to find it

Trees **Bushes** **Grass** **Water** **Sky**

What part of the animal kingdom it belongs to

Amphibian **Bird** **Fish** **Invertebrate** **Mammal** **Reptile**

BACKYARD BIOLOGIST REFERENCE SHEET

Good explorers take the time to study and understand the creatures that they are observing. Below are some of the terms that will help you better understand the creatures you might discover in your backyard or local park.

WHAT THEY ARE

Living Organism
An organism that is alive. They can move on their own, grow, require food to survive, and respond to things around them. An example of a living organism is YOU!

Non-Living Organism
Organisms that aren't alive. They can't move or grow, they don't require food, and don't respond to things around them. A rock is a non-living organism.

Warm-Blooded
Warm-blooded animals can make their own body heat even when it is cold outside. Whether it is really hot or really cold, warm-blooded animals have body temperatures that usually stay the same. Mammals and birds are warm-blooded.

Cold-Blooded
Cold-blooded animals become hotter and colder, depending on the temperature outside. When it's cold outside, their body functions slow down, and when it's warm, they speed up. Amphibians, reptiles, fish, and invertebrates are cold-blooded.

Animal Kingdom
All organisms in the Animal Kingdom share three characteristics:
1) they eat plants or other animals,
2) they are able to move on their own, and
3) they have more than one cell.
There are six different groups within the Animal Kingdom:

Amphibians - All amphibians have backbones, porous skin, are cold-blooded, and have four legs. Examples of amphibians are frogs, toads, and salamanders.

Birds - All birds have backbones, feathers, are warm-blooded, and their babies are born in eggs. Examples of birds are cardinals, ostriches, and ducks.

Fish - All fish have backbones, live in water, are cold-blooded, and use fins to move. Examples of fish are goldfish, sharks, and tuna.

Invertebrates - This is the largest of the kingdoms, with more invertebrates than all the other kingdoms combined. Invertebrates don't have backbones, are cold-blooded, some live on land, and some live in water. Examples of invertebrates are insects, lobsters, and worms.

Mammals - All mammals have backbones, hair, are warm-blooded, and their babies are born alive. Examples of mammals are cats, dogs, seals, and YOU!

Reptiles - All reptiles have backbones, scales, are cold-blooded, and their babies are born in eggs. Examples of reptiles are turtles, lizards, snakes, and alligators.

WHERE THEY LIVE

Ecosystem
An ecosystem is made up of all of the living and nonliving organisms in an area.

Habitat
This is where an animal lives and includes everything around it such as plants, food, water, and other creatures.

Range
This is where an animal can be found during its lifetime.

Native Species
Living organisms that live in an area naturally and haven't been put there by people.

Introduced Species
Living organisms that can be found in an area, but are not native to it.

Invasive Species
A non-native species that disturbs the ecosystems in which it has been introduced.

HOW THEY LOOK

Physical Traits
How a creature looks such as its color, if it has wings, fur, or scales, and its size. Paying attention to how a creature looks will help you identify it.

Camouflage
Coloring that helps a creature blend into its surroundings, making it difficult to see. For example, some lizards are green, the same color of the bushes they live in.

Polymorphism
When a species can be found in different colors in the same range.

Dimorphism - When a male and female of the same species look different such as color or size.

HOW THEY ACT

Life Cycle
A life cycle is a series of changes that happens to all living things during its life. For instance, a toad's life cycle begins as a fertilized egg. The egg develops into a tadpole, which grows until it becomes a toad. During your life cycle, you grow from a baby to an adult.

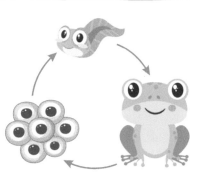

Food Chain
Food chain describes the order in which organisms in an ecosystem depend on each other for food. For example, in your backyard, caterpillars eat plants, dragonflies eat caterpillars, and birds eat dragonflies.

Metamorphosis
This is when an organism changes from one distinct form to another as it grows. An example in your backyard is a caterpillar changing into a butterfly.

Migration
Migration is the seasonal movement of creatures from one place to another. For example, some birds and butterflies migrate each fall from the United States to Mexico, coming back to the US in the spring.

Hibernation

Winter can be hard for animals. It's cold and food can be hard to find. Some animals hibernate during the winter, which is kind of like sleeping for several months. While animals hibernate, their body slows down and survives on the animal's stored body fat.

Dormancy

This is similar to hibernation, but the animal doesn't sleep continually. Their body slows down and they move around less, often only coming out of their den or burrow to eat.

Brumation

This is another, special kind of hibernation that cold-blooded animals use. If it gets cold, their body is forced to slow down and they can't digest food. Once the weather warms up again, they become active and can eat.

Instinctual Behavior

This is a behavior that an animal doesn't have to learn and is shared by all the members of a species.

Learned Behavior

This is a behavior that has to be learned, like adult owls teaching their babies how to hunt for food.

Colonies

Colonies are groups of organisms of one species that live and interact closely with each other.

Shelter

Shelters are what people and animals use to protect themselves from their surroundings while they sleep and raise their babies.

Diurnal

Creatures that are active during the day and sleep at night.

Nocturnal

Creatures that are active at night and sleep during the day.

Omnivore

An omnivore is an organism that regularly consumes different types of food including plants and animals.

Herbivore

Creatures that eat primarily plants.

Carnivore

Creatures that eat primarily meat.

Pollination

This is when pollen grains are transferred from one plant to another helping them reproduce. Many insects, like bees, are pollinators.

Venom

A poisonous substance created by certain creatures such as snakes, that is transmitted to a victim by a bite or sting.

Toxin

A poisonous substance that causes harm when it enters the body or touches the skin. Some creatures, like caterpillars, have toxins on their skin.

HOW TO LEARN ABOUT CREATURES

Observation

This is learning about an organism by watching it, and how it behaves in its environment.

Investigation

This is learning about an organism by reading about it in books or on the internet.

SCREECH OWL

EASTERN SCREECH OWL

Explorer Tips

Look at the trees around your backyard because you never know what you might discover! This Screech Owl has made a nest for its family in a hole it found high up in a tree.

ACTIVITY: Make a map of your backyard or park and mark all the trees that have holes larger than your fist. Check it regularly, especially in the spring, to see if any birds go in and out. Be sure to stay still and quiet, so you don't upset the mommy and daddy bird and their new babies.

  Year Round

 Nocturnal

Trees

Bird

Screech Owls live in every state and don't migrate. They will live around people, and if you put an owl box in your yard, you might have a family of screech owls move in during the spring and raise a family.

Lifespan
8-10 years

Size
7" tall = Scissors

Weight
6 ounces = D Battery

Favorite Food
Carnivore
Small rodents

NATURE NOTES

Screech Owls are nocturnal, hunting at night and sleeping during the day. They like to make their home in holes found in trees. During the day, you might be able to see one with its head peeking out and enjoying a little sunshine. You'll have to look close though, because the owl's feathers are great camouflage, helping it to blend in with the trees where it lives and hide from predators.

FUN FACTS

Screech Owls can be found in different colors depending on where they live. Southern owls tend to be grey or red and northern owls tend to be mostly grey or brown. When the same species can be found in the same region in different colors, it is called "polymorphism". These changes in the color of their feathers help the birds to blend into their specific habitat and keeps them safe from predators.

RED MORPH SCREECH OWL

WASP

RED WASP

Explorer Tips

Many creatures, like wasps and bees, protect themselves against things that might hurt them with "stingers". These stingers, found on the back of their bodies, allow them to inject a liquid called "venom" into other creatures. Stings and venom can hurt. Wasps and bees aren't mean and they don't want to sting you, but they will if they feel like you might hurt them. If you see a wasp or bee, don't swat at it. Instead, move away very slowly, and they will probably fly off and not bother you.

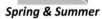
Spring & Summer

Diurnal

Bushes

Invertebrate

Wasps are very common backyard insects that you can see flying around in the spring and summer. They sometimes build their nests under the roof of houses and buildings.

Lifespan
2-4 weeks

Size
1" long = Bottle Cap

Weight
.003 ounces = 3 Raindrops

Favorite Food
Omnivore
Caterpillars, insects, and nectar from flowers

NATURE NOTES

Wasps come in just about every color, but the most common backyard wasps are red, yellow, black, or brown. Some wasps live by themselves, and some live in groups called colonies. Wasps are good to have in your yard because they eat many insects that destroy gardens. Plus they are excellent pollinators. They enjoy nectar from flowers and help spread pollen, which is important in helping flowering plants grow.

FUN FACTS

Wasps build nests to sleep in and raise their babies. They use plants, bark, and wood that they chew up into a soft substance called pulp. This is very similar to the way people make paper. These nests look like a honeycomb and can hold as many as 15,000 adult and baby wasps! If you see a wasp nest, don't get too close or try to touch it, or you might get stung!

SKUNK

STRIPED SKUNK

Explorer Tips

At night your backyard turns into a completely different world.
ACTIVITY: *Ask your parents if you can have a camp out in your backyard. Spring and summer are some of the best times to pitch your tent to listen and enjoy the sounds of nature because this is when many creatures are most active. You might hear the crickets chirping, owls hooting, and critters walking around looking for an evening snack. If you leave a dim light on and sit very quietly, you might even see a skunk go wandering by.*

Year Round

Nocturnal

Grass

Mammal

Skunks can be found all over the United States and usually live their whole life in the same area. They live comfortably around people with as many as a dozen skunks living in an average neighborhood.

Lifespan
3 years

Size
20" long = Cat

Weight
8 pounds = Gallon of Milk

Favorite Food
Omnivore
Small mammals, insects, and fruit

NATURE NOTES

Skunks protect themselves by lifting their tail and spraying a very stinky liquid! This spray can go up to 10 feet, and you can smell it as far as 1½ miles away. It's so stinky that even big animals, like bears, will leave skunks alone! They will only use their spray as a last resort. If they feel scared, they will try growling, spitting, and fluffing up their fur, but, if all else fails, watch out for that stinky protection!

FUN FACTS

Skunks make their homes in lots of different places including holes in or under trees, brush piles, holes in the ground called burrows (that they dig with their sharp claws), and even under houses. Skunks don't hibernate during the winter, but they do become less active. They sleep more, their body temperature drops, and they only going out at night for food. This is called a dormant state.

THERE MIGHT BE A SKUNK LIVING IN THIS HOLE UNDER A TREE

LADY BEETLE

SPOTLESS LADY BEETLE

Explorer Tips

Exploring is best when done with a friend because the more sets of ears and eyes you have for the hunt, the more luck you'll have discovering unique and interesting creatures. Ask a brother or sister, a friend, or your parents to go with you when you start exploring. Sharing what you find with others makes the adventure that much more fun!

ACTIVITY: *Have a contest to see who can find the most creatures.*

Spring & Summer

Diurnal

Bushes

Invertebrate

Lady Beetles can be found in almost every habitat in the United States. In areas where it gets cold in the winter, these beetles will brumate (similar to hibernation) in large groups for up to 9 months.

Lifespan
1 year

Size
1/2" long = Asprin/Pill

Weight
.001 ounces = Raindrop

Favorite Food
Carnivore
Aphids

NATURE NOTES

Lady Beetles are solid red or red with black spots. When threatened, they secrete a yucky-tasting fluid that keeps predators from eating them. They are considered good bugs to have in your yard and garden because they eat other insects that eat garden plants, such as aphids. Many gardeners use Lady Beetles, rather than chemicals, as an environmentally friendly way to control the harmful insects that can damage or destroy their plants.

FUN FACTS

Another beetle that you might find in your yard or park is an Asian Lady Beetle. These insects are "invasive", which means they aren't a natural occurring member of an ecosystem. The Asian Lady Beetle competes with native Lady Beetles for food and territory, and scientists believe that they have helped cause the decline in populations of native Lady Beetles in the United States.

ASIAN LADY BEETLE

GARTER SNAKE

Explorer Tips

A good explorer watches where they walk! If you're exploring in an area with long grass, be sure and watch where you step because you never know what might be moving around in the grass!

ACTIVITY: Small creatures like mice and snakes hide in tall grass along with lots of different bugs, so walk slowly and pay attention to your surroundings. What creatures can you see peeking at you through the grass?

Year Round

Nocturnal and Diurnal

Grass

Reptile

Garter Snakes are common snakes that live throughout the United States and enjoy places that are close to water like the areas around ponds, marshes, and lakes.

Lifespan
10 years

Size
24" long = Table Lamp

Weight
5 ounces = Baseball

Favorite Food
Carnivore
Frogs, insects, and rodents

NATURE NOTES

Garter Snakes come in lots of different colors, but almost all of them have three stripes running the length of their bodies. They also have tongues that are two colors: half red and half black. They live on the ground and are very shy. They can swim and even climb trees and bushes if they feel threatened. Their bite isn't poisonous, but they might bite if they get scared so if you see one, look but don't touch.

FUN FACTS

Snakes and other reptiles are all "cold-blooded", which means that, unlike you, their body can't produce its own body heat, so they have to rely on their environment to stay warm. When it's warm outside, they are active, and when it's cold, they are slow and sluggish. This is why you might find cold-blooded creatures, like snakes, sitting in the sun as they try to warm up their bodies.

DIAMONDBACK WATER SNAKE SUNNING ITSELF

CATERPILLAR

**WHITE-MARKED TUSSOCK
MOTH CATERPILLAR**

Explorer Tips

Just because a creature is cute and furry doesn't mean you should try to touch or hold it like you would your pet dog or cat. Many creatures have toxins on their skin or fur to help protect them from other creatures that might hurt them. Fuzzy caterpillars, for example, have a toxin on the fuzzy parts of their body that can cause your skin to hurt, itch, or get a rash on it if you touch or try to hold them.

ACTIVITY: *Practice looking but not touching things you see in nature.*

Spring & Summer

Nocturnal

Bushes

Invertebrate

Caterpillars are common all over the world. You can find them in trees and bushes eating leaves. They can make silk, so you might even find them hanging in the air from branches.

Lifespan
2-5 weeks

Size
2"-3" long = Eraser

Weight
.1 ounces = Penny

Favorite Food
Herbivore
Leaves and plants

NATURE NOTES

A caterpillar has one job: to eat! They use the food they eat to store enough energy so that they can transform from a caterpillar into a moth or butterfly. They are more active at night, but you still might find them eating or moving around in bushes during the day. Caterpillars come in just about every color of the rainbow, and their color usually comes from the food they eat, which helps them to blend into their surroundings.

FUN FACTS

Not all caterpillars you see will one day turn into butterflies. Most fuzzy caterpillars will one day become a moth, while most smooth caterpillars become butterflies. Moths look similar to butterflies, but are active at night rather than in the day. Also, when they rest, their wings are spread flat. When butterflies rest, they usually hold their wings straight up.

MOTH - ITS WINGS ARE LAYING FLAT ON THE LEAF

BUMBLEBEE

TRI-COLORED BUMBLEBEE

Explorer Tips

The kingdom in your backyard is always changing. When you explore your backyard in winter you might only discover a few birds. When you explore in spring it will be completely different with all kinds of insects, reptiles, and birds flying and crawling around.

ACTIVITY: Explore you backyard every few days and make a list of everything you see. What creatures are different and what creatures are new?

Bumblebees can be found in just about every habitat and ecosystem in the United States. Tri-Colored Bumblebees can be found in the Northeastern part of the United States.

Spring, Summer, and Fall

Diurnal

Bushes

Invertebrate

Lifespan
6 months

Size
1/2" long = Asprin/Pill

Weight
.03 ounces = Small Paperclip

Favorite Food
Herbivore
Nectar

NATURE NOTES

If you ever see a fuzzy insect flying around your flowers, you might be seeing a Bumblebee. Bumblebees live in small colonies in holes under the ground. Just like Honey Bees, they eat nectar and are important insects in their ecosystems because they are pollinators. This means they move pollen from one plant to another, which plants need to grow. Bumblebees make honey, but only enough to feed the other bumblebees in their colony.

FUN FACTS

Unlike Bumblebees, honey bees are not native to North America. They were introduced in the 1700s and have become an important part of the ecosystem and economy. They live in much larger colonies than bumblebees and make more honey then the colony needs. This extra honey can be removed from the hive and sold in stores. So the next time you enjoy honey on your toast, you have a honey bee to thank!

HONEY BEE

TOAD

GULF COAST TOAD

Explorer Tips

Many animals, like toads, might make their homes in holes and other nooks and crannies around your house.

ACTIVITY: *When you're looking for creatures in your yard, be sure to look down low for places toads and other animals can wiggle in to. Look in brush piles, around leaves, and even at holes and cracks in sidewalks and concrete structures. This toad made his burrow under some wood planks. He wiggles into it through in a small hole in the wood.*

Spring & Summer

Nocturnal

Grass

Amphibian

Toads live in many habitats. Most like to live in areas that are moist, like under leaves and logs or in a burrow under concrete patios and sidewalks. In cold climates, they brumate during the winter.

Lifespan
8-10 years

Size
2"-3" tall = Eraser

Weight
2 ounces = Tennis Ball

Favorite Food
Carnivore
Ants, small insects, mammals, and reptiles

NATURE NOTES

Toads come in lots of different colors and sizes, but most are brownish green, which helps them blend in with their surroundings. Unlike frogs, toads don't need to live in or near water. They're nocturnal (sleep during the day) and come out at night to forage for food. Their dry and bumpy skin is covered with a special toxin to protect them from predators. It can cause a rash on your hands if you pick one up, so remember to look and not touch.

FUN FACTS

Toads live their lives in three stages and in two completely different environments. They start out as eggs that the female lays in water. When they hatch, they are called tadpoles. Tadpoles have tails and breathe air like a fish. When they grow up, they become toads. Their tail goes away, they grow legs, and they move to a life on the land where they breathe air. This change of shape is called metamorphosis.

TADPOLES

RACCOON

Explorer Tips

Many of the critters or creatures who live in your backyard are nocturnal, which means they sleep during the day and are active at night. Many of these creatures wake up as the sun is going down.

ACTIVITY: Grab a flashlight and ask your parents to explore your backyard with you before you go to bed. Many creatures will be out and about right after the sun goes down. You might stand still against a tree or wall and see what crosses your path.

Year Round

Nocturnal

Grass

Mammal

Raccoons are highly adaptable animals and can be found in many different habitats and ecosystems. Traditionally an animal of the forest, they have adapted to be comfortable living in neighborhoods.

Lifespan
2-3 years

Size
12" tall = Notebook

Weight
18 pounds = 2 Gallons of Milk

Favorite Food
Omnivore
Fruit, vegetables, insects, eggs, and seeds

NATURE NOTES

Raccoons are incredibly smart and adaptable animals. When they live around people, they sleep during the day in trees, caves, burrows, under houses and even in attics. They don't hibernate in the winter, and their heavy fur coat keeps them warm when it gets cold outsided4. Their strong sense of smell and excellent eyesight helps them forage for food at night although, especially in the spring, you might see one out and about during the day.

FUN FACTS

Raccoons are probably the smartest creature that you'll discover in your backyard or park! In fact, scientists believe that they might be as smart as monkeys. They are very good at solving complex problems, such as opening enclosures to get to food. The most sensitive part of their body are their hands which they use for grabbing things, opening containers, and even opening doors!

ASSASSIN BUG

MILKWEED ASSASSIN BUG

Explorer Tips

A good explorer respects nature! You share your yard with lots of different critters and creatures, and so it's important to give them their space. You never know if a creature you find will bite or if its skin or fur has a toxin on it that can make you sick or your skin itch.

ACTIVITY: *When you go out to discover the different critters and creatures in your yard or park, remember to look and not touch or pick up what you find, even if it's a tiny assassin bug!*

Year Round

Diurnal

Bushes

Invertebrate

Assassin Bugs are common insects in gardens all over the United States. They live in lots of different habitats. Look for Assassin Bugs in your yard crawling around bushes and plants.

Lifespan
1 year

Size
1" long = Bottle Cap

Weight
.001 ounces = Raindrop

Favorite Food
Carnivore
Small insects, moths, and caterpillars

NATURE NOTES

Assassin Bugs have a three-stage life cycle: from egg to nymph to adult. The nymphs look like adult assassin bugs, except they don't have wings. When fully grown, the adults use their wings to slowly fly around bushes looking for food. They generally leave people alone, but might bite if you touch or try to hold them. These insects are often used as natural pest controls in garden ecosystems because they kill other insects that eat plants.

FUN FACTS

Assassin Bugs don't have teeth or large mouths. Instead, they drink their food through what looks like a built-in straw on the end of their head. They use this "straw" to inject a venom into the bug that they capture. This venom turns the bug's insides into liquid, and the Assassin Bug slurps up its meal. So, the next time you drink with a straw, you'll be acting just like the Assassin Bug!

MILKWEED ASSASSIN BUG NYMPH

HOUSE FINCH

Explorer Tips

ACTIVITY: *A great way to encourage birds and other creatures to visit your backyard is to put out bird feeders and plant flowers and bushes to give visiting birds and bugs a place to hide and look for food. Plants that are native to your region are always the best choice. Also, different birds enjoy different foods at your feeders. Some birds eat seeds and nuts, some eat peanut butter, and some birds, like finches, will come into a feeder that's filled with sunflower or thistle seeds.*

Year Round

Diurnal

Trees

Bird

House Finches are common backyard birds throughout the United States. In fact, they might come visit your yard if you put black oil sunflower seeds out for them.

Lifespan
10 years

Size
6" tall = Dollar Bill

Weight
.8 ounces = AA Battery

Favorite Food
Herbivore
Seeds

NATURE NOTES

House finches are social birds that like to travel with other finches in groups called flocks. Traveling in flocks is one way for birds to protect themselves from predators. Most finches stay year-round in the same location. Some finches, who live in places where it gets cold in the winter, will fly south to warmer climates. This is called migration. One of the reasons birds and other creatures migrate is to travel to places where it is easier to find food.

FUN FACTS

Once or twice a year, birds lose their feathers and new ones grow in. This is called molting. Generally, male House Finches have red and tan feathers, but their coloring can range from yellow to orange to bright red. This change in color is caused by what the bird eats during its molt. Females are much more attracted to the bright red males, believing that these males will be better able to feed their babies.

JUMPING SPIDER

REGAL JUMPING SPIDER

Explorer Tips

Many of the creatures you will discover in your backyard kingdom are cold-blooded. This means that they need warm weather to help them move. When it's cold out, like early in the morning, these creatures don't move very quickly so they are much easier to find and watch.
ACTIVITY: *Set your alarm clock this weekend and plan to get up early for an adventure before breakfast. You'll be amazed at what you'll discover.*

Year Round

Nocturnal

Bushes

Invertebrate

Jumping Spiders can be found in just about every habitat and environment. Don't be surprised if you see them lurking on fences, trees, and bushes looking for a tasty treat.

Lifespan
1-2 years

Size
1/2" long = Aspirin

Weight
.006 ounces = 3 Raindrops

Favorite Food
Carnivore
Small insects

NATURE NOTES

Jumping Spiders are welcomed backyard critters as they eat insect pests. They range in size from as small as the tip of a pencil to as large as your fingernail. The Regal Jumping Spider is the largest jumping spider in the U.S. and they are generally calm and comfortable around people. In fact, some people even keep them as pets! However, if they feel threatened, they will bite so remember, if you see a spider, look but don't touch!

FUN FACTS

Some spiders are passive hunters. They make webs to catch food that comes to them. Jumping Spiders are active hunters. They don't use webs, they literally jump on their prey! They have eight eyes, allowing them to look all around them without moving, and can jump up to 50 times their body length! When they spot a small insect, they jump and subdue the insect with a venom-filled bite.

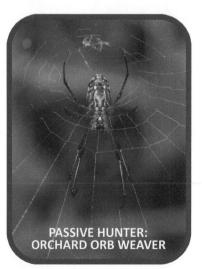

**PASSIVE HUNTER:
ORCHARD ORB WEAVER**

SQUIRREL

EASTERN GREY SQUIRREL

Explorer Tips

Your ears are one of your best explorer tools. Creatures work hard to blend into their surroundings, and sometimes the best way to find a creature in your backyard or park is to listen for it.

ACTIVITY: Close your eyes and listen to the sounds around you. Once you hear a creature making a chirp or buzz, use your ears to help your eyes "follow" the sound until you find the critter making the noise. Remember to be still so you don't scare it.

Year Round

Diurnal

Trees

Mammal

Squirrels can be found throughout the US. They can easily be seen in the trees around neighborhoods and parks. If you listen, sometimes you can hear them chattering in the trees.

Lifespan
8-10 years

Size
12" tall = Notebook

Weight
2 pounds = Two Soccer Balls

Favorite Food
Herbivore
Nuts and seeds

NATURE NOTES

Squirrels are very smart animals that live in trees in forests, parks, and neighborhoods. They are one of the few animals that are diurnal, active during the day, rather than nocturnal, active at night. Most of the squirrels that you'll find in your backyard or park are gray or brown with long, bushy tails. Sometimes they have white or tan bellies. Their coloring provides camouflage and helps them blend into the trees and hide from predators.

FUN FACTS

Squirrels are herbivores, which means they don't eat meat. In fact, they love nuts such as acorns! Squirrels will often bury some of the nuts they find to eat later, and, occasionally, they will forget where those nuts are buried. Eventually those buried nuts grow into healthy trees. Scientists believe that 1 out of every 3 trees in the forest was "planted" by a squirrel!

LIZARD

WESTERN FENCE LIZARD

Explorer Tips

Many animals, like lizards, have special coloring that helps them to blend in to their surroundings, making it hard for predators to see and find them. This is called "camouflage".

ACTIVITY: *When you're looking for critters and creatures in your yard, be sure and study tree trunks, piles of leaves, and branches looking for movement. If you pay close attention, you might discover a critter that has such good camouflage that it's able to hide right in plain site!*

Year Round

Diurnal

Bushes

Reptile

Lizards live all over the United States and in just about every habitat. If they live in places that get cold in the winter, they brumate until it warms up. Lizards in warm climates are active year round.

Lifespan
15-20 years

Size
7" long = Scissors

Weight
.4 ounces = AAA Battery

Favorite Food
Carnivore
Small insects

NATURE NOTES

There are over 6,000 different lizard species in the world in every color of the rainbow. Most lizards you'll see in your yard will be brown or green to match their habitat. You'll see them moving around the ground, sitting in bushes, hanging out on walls, and even climbing trees. They can move very fast, but on chilly days, since they're cold-blooded and need heat to move, you might see them relaxing and warming up in the sun.

FUN FACTS

Lizards have lots of different ways to protect themselves from predators. Some have camouflage coloring that helps them blend into their environment, some can change the color of their skin depending on where they are, and most lizards can lose their tail if they are attacked and grabbed by their tail, helping them to get away. But don't worry, their tail will grow back!

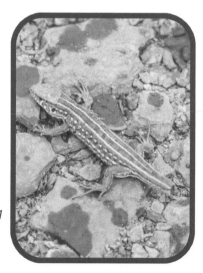

PILL BUG

Explorer Tips

You never know where you might find a fascinating critter when you start exploring!

ACTIVITY: Look along the area where the grass meets the sidewalk; look at the grass for things moving between the blades; look around the areas close to your house; look under stairs. Remember to be careful if you lift up leaves, a piece of wood, or other items you find on the ground because you never know what might be hiding underneath it.

Year Round

Nocturnal

Grass

Invertebrate

Pill Bugs are very busy crawling around at night looking for food, and they like to sleep during the day. If you're careful, you might find a Pill Bug taking a nap under some leaves in your yard.

Lifespan
2 years

Size
1/2" long = Aspirin

Weight
.002 ounces = 2 Raindrops

Favorite Food
Herbivore
Dead leaves
and wood

NATURE NOTES

Pill Bugs have a dark brown or black body that looks like it's put together from different, overlapping pieces. They like to live in places where it's damp, like under the ground, leaves, and dead logs. They are important to the ecosystem because they eat dead leaves and wood. If a Pill Bug gets scared or thinks something is going to hurt it, it will roll into a ball to protect itself. That's why some people call them "rolly polly bugs".

FUN FACTS

If you see a Pill Bug crawling around, you might think it's an insect like a wasp or an ant, but they are actually more like a lobster! Pill Bugs are part of the invertebrate family, but are not insects, they are crustaceans. Crustaceans are invertebrates that live in the water such as shrimp, crabs, and lobster. Pill Bugs are the only crustaceans that live their entire lives on land.

WOODPECKER

RED-BELLIED WOODPECKER

Explorer Tips

Not all birds that visit your backyard will eat the seeds at your bird feeders. Many birds will spend their time bouncing around trees and bushes looking for a tasty meal of bugs and spiders.

ACTIVITY: When exploring in your backyard or local park, be sure and look at the trees, and you'll be amazed at what you discover! The best way to spot birds is to look for movement in the branches and leaves and you might see a bird peek out.

Year Round

Diurnal

Trees

Bird

Woodpeckers are very common backyard birds that can be found in many different habitats and ecosystems. Red-Bellied Woodpeckers live in the eastern half of the country, but different species can be found throughout the US.

Lifespan
12 years

Size
9" long = Envelope

Weight
2.4 ounces = C Battery

Favorite Food
Omnivore
Insects, seeds, nuts, fruit, and sap

NATURE NOTES

If you ever hear a "tap... tap... tap...", chances are you're hearing a woodpecker looking for food. These interesting birds eat insects, and they use their long, pointed bill to tap into tree bark and reach into tight spaces to find insects to eat. They also use their bills to chisel holes into trees to make nests and to communicate with other woodpeckers. These woodpeckers don't migrate, but spend their entire lives in the same general area.

FUN FACTS

For some bird species the male and female look exactly alike, and for others, the male and female look completely different or have different coloring. When the male and female look different, it's called "dimorphism". For these Red-Bellied Woodpeckers, the male has more red on its head than the female. This extra coloring is used to help the male attract a female mate.

FEMALE RED-BELLIED WOODPECKER

DRAGONFLY

BLUE DASHER DRAGONFLY

Explorer Tips

Many creatures, like dragonflies, will find a spot that they like and keep coming back to it.

ACTIVITY: *If you see a dragonfly, stand very still and watch where it lands. If you move slowly towards it and it flies off, stand very still and there's a good chance it will come back and land in the same area. By slowly creeping forward, stopping, and creeping forward, you might get close enough to get a good look at its amazing coloring.*

 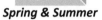
Spring & Summer

Diurnal

Bushes

Invertebrate

Dragonflies can be found all over the United States. Nymphs are found in ponds and marshes. Adult dragonflies can be found in almost every habitat.

Lifespan
5 years

Size
3" long = Crayon

Weight
.1 ounce = Penny

Favorite Food
Carnivore
Flies, ants, bees, and other small insects

NATURE NOTES

Dragonflies can be found in just about every color you can imagine. Even though they have legs, they can't walk. They do everything while flying including catching their food. They are excellent flyers and can move up, down, backwards, and forwards, just like a helicopter, and fly up to 35 miles per hour. They have huge eyes and can see all the way around them at the same time, which helps them catch other flying insects.

FUN FACTS

Dragonflies have several different forms during their life cycle. Female dragonflies lay their eggs in ponds or marshes, which hatch a few days later, into nymphs. Nymphs live in the water and breathe air through gills, like a fish. They will live as nymphs for up to 4 years, shedding their skin several times as they grow. Eventually, they shed their skin a final time and live life on land as a mature dragonfly.

FEMALE DRAGONFLY LAYING HER EGGS IN A POND

OPOSSUM

Explorer Tips

When you go out to explore, remember to change into your play clothes, and don't be afraid to get dirty! Sometimes, to find and get a good look at the creatures and critters in your backyard, you need to lay on your belly or crawl around in the grass. Be sure and ask your parents before you go exploring to make sure you have on the right explorer clothes.

Year Round

Nocturnal

Trees

Mammal

Opossums usually spend their entire life in the same area and are common where people live. They sleep during the day in trees, in holes under ground, and even under houses.

Lifespan
1-2 years

Size
30" long = Medium Sized Dog

Weight
10 pounds = Cat

Favorite Food
Omnivore
Small rodents, insects, birds, fruits, and nuts

NATURE NOTES

Opossums are marsupials and have pouches, like kangaroos, where their babies stay until they're grown. They use their long tails to help hold on to branches when they're climbing trees. They are comfortable living around people and are a very important part of your backyard habitat because they eat rodents such as mice and rats! They generally leave people alone, but might hiss and snap if they feel scared.

FUN FACTS

Opossums have a very unique way of protecting themselves from predators–they pretend that they are dead! If an Opossum feels like something is going to hurt it, it will fall over, let it's mouth open up and tongue hang out, will keep its eyes open but not moving, and stay very still. Then, its body will make a stinky smell just like it's dead. It can pretend to be dead for several hours.

AN OPOSSUM PRETENDING TO BE DEAD

CERTIFICATE OF ACHIEVEMENT

Having completed the necessary course study,
this is to certify that

_____

Is an official

Junior
Backyard Biologist

The Fun Continues with FREE ACTIVITY PACKS

Based on the concepts and creatures introduced in this book, this free activity pack is designed to continue your child's adventure of exploration and discovery in nature.

Scan the QR Code to download your
Free Activity Packs
or visit CherylJohnsonAuthor.com

Introduce your students to the beauty of nature with a

School Visit and Nature Presentation

by author and nature photographer
Cheryl Johnson

Fun and
Educational
Author
Visits
to Your
School

Visit CherylJohnsonAuthor.com or scan
the QR Code below to learn more!

About The Author

Cheryl wears many hats: she's a business owner, photographer, and author; more importantly, she's a wife, mother, sister, and friend. During the day, she can be found running a boutique advertising agency, developing marketing campaigns, producing television commercials, and designing print material for customers. In the evenings, she puts on her wife and momma hat, enjoying life with her husband, two daughters, and their dog. On the weekends, she can often be found with camera in hand, exploring the wilds of nature and adding images to her award-winning photography portfolio. In between all this craziness, she loves to squeeze in some time to sit at her computer to write and design books for children and adults.

"I believe very strongly that you need to follow your passions," she says. "Everything I've ever done, I've been very passionate about, although, often, completely unprepared for. My degree is in Religious Studies, yet I ended up in a career in advertising. One day I picked up a camera and decided to take wildlife photos. Several years later, my pictures are winning awards. In 2019, I decided to try my hand at writing a children's book. The result, "My Backyard Bird Book", was picked up by a publisher and has gone on to sell tens of thousands of copies. I think the biggest lesson I've learned on this crazy journey called 'Life' is that you can't be afraid to take chances. Certainly, I've failed at many things over the course of my life and career, but I've also succeeded at many things, and because I've always followed paths that bring me joy, whether I've succeeded or failed, I've always had the best time!"

If you would like to enjoy more of her photography, please "LIKE" her Facebook page, "Backyard Bird Nerd", for a daily dose of nature cuteness!

Printed in the USA
CPSIA information can be obtained
at www.ICGtesting.com
LVHW072048040923
757051LV00059B/597